SPILLED THOUGHTS

THE THINGS I NEVER SAY

DESHAUN PRICE

CONTENTS

Fun times

It's funny how the past creeps up on you...

And suddenly the present moment goes

from a gift to an unfortunate curse...

Your happy place tainted by reminiscent thoughts...

And the thought of it all just makes matters worse...

Now those smiles shared under the star filled sky

are stale frowns when the sunlight peeks over the horizon...

Mind racing like it's a game of truth or dare...

Torn between your heart and your guilty conscious...

You're having a hard time deciding...

Dare to continue to be you...

Or be set free by finally sharing the truth...

Thrown into a lose lose situation...

Life's true meaning of a catch twenty two...

Fun times right...

Joke's on whoever told you just live life...

Besides you're single and young...

But the laughter eventually comes to a screeching halt...

And all those fun times are finally done

I'm just a writer

I'm just a writer of poetry...
However I remember a while back when I used rap...
Don't look so confused by that notion...
It was just poetic lines linked to the sounds of the boom...
boom...
clap...
But now the drums I was so accustomed to are replaced
by blaring silence...
Hell finger snaps are usually my chorus at times
when I'm needing guidance...
And because reciting verses behind a mic was once
a passion of mine...
You can see the rhythmic patterns of my stanzas...
And kinda hear the instrumentals playing in your mind...
Now I'm just writing to the beat of my own solo drum...
One stanza is a boom...
Next one is a tap...
I write and write until the beat is finally done...
So either transcribed through your eyes...
Or transferred from my voice to your ears...
I'm forever writing to that silent beat you can't help
but hear...

It's cool...you can read it out loud to catch the beat this time

That love

Ever sat and gave thought to the comment or
reply of I love you too?...
Like really think about...
Just the formation of the sentence seems like it's another
thing to good to be true...
Circumstantial statement...
Sometimes conditional at best...
Feels like the only way you'll love me first is if I pass the test...
Or am I tripping?...
Do you not hold tight to the notion of he should
say it first?...
Or maybe it's the "I'm the prize" feeling...
Or just over estimating your worth?...
Don't get me wrong...
I for one believe finding a wife is the ultimate goal...
But I feel like if your pride keeps your feelings buried...
Then somehow you're playing a role...
Either you want this love thing...
Or you want the image of it all...
Day one or seventeen hundred and twenty...
It's ultimately your call

Spilled Thoughts

The deception of spilled thoughts had me ready to dive
right in...
Little did I know it was pieces of left over conversations
you were having in your sleep with him...
Your resting conscious reminding you that I'm just not him
and he's nowhere near me...
Nuances detected in your "this topic is not about you"
dialect...
Forced me to bite the harsh reality of truth...
I'm just not HE...
But on the other end of the spectrum...
You're forced to accept the fact...
He's just not into you...
Met at the same place where we all find ourselves
asking where we went stupid...
Trying to run away from one heartbreak
while unknowingly chasing another...
Thinking your last train to happiness departed with the
garbage bag of bleached clothes you left outside the door...
Good thing I got my own...
Yep...correct in knowing I'm not like that brother...
So far from being him...
Yet this ecstasy that I provide is levels above things
he could do...

The entirety of your dealings was invested in his interest...

Whatever happened to him thinking about you...

No more I me and mine...

Especially when we us and ours sound so much better...

Why get caught up in circumstantial love shit...

When I have a heart built to love you through whatever...

FORD tough...

Everything I had came out the mud...

But no worries I got us on lock...

Overtime...I learned that sunshine and mud made

that same mud turn to rock...

I'm just tryna be something solid!!

It's you

I wanted to hand you the stars but they just seemed
so far out of reach...
And as time passed grasping for the moon seemed
like constant defeat...
I just seen something in you that for me finally
made the world make sense...
Gazing into your eyes as the clouds shifted by me...
Everything else was pushed to the past tense...
Got me so focused on the future...
The right now moments don't stand a fighting chance...
Trust me dear...
For I understand the hesitation and fear
of moving forward...
But that's common doubt all at first glance...
This here...
This is something that your heart beats to...
That feeling that you think only movies could provide...
So to whom ever told you real love doesn't exist...
Middle finger to that person who lied...
Was only a plot twist stated to mess with your proceed
with caution mental...
If you could find the courage to disregard that...
I will personally show you how this love thing could be
oh so simple...

Effort...

That's numero uno on the list...

And once that's mastered the rest of the challenges tend

to go something like this...

Compromising in moments you'd rather just give up...

In the darkest days and you're feeling down...

I'm the guiding light to lift you up...

You have my back...

And I got your everything...

Plus so much more...

Me rooting for your success...

Turned into a lifetime of us building this dynasty

with love at the core...

Above all else...

Trusting that no matter what...

WE ARE IN THIS TOGETHER...

Take heed of my actions and not just the words...

When I say I GOT YOU...

THAT MEANS I GOT YOU FOREVER

The REWARD is usually GREATER than the RISK...

Second chances don't always come along like this...

Make the MOST OF IT

Training Day

Went into this new life convinced I was light years pass
my childhood trauma...
Moved forward with little to no clue how easily I'm triggered
by the slightest of drama...
Trained to smile in public...
And cry the moment I find myself in private...
Stand bold in my "Im not bothered" face...
Knowing damn well how hard things could probably get...
Never let em see me fold...
And I for sure can't withstand the backlash if by chance
I would break...
So with masks to cover the scars and pain of my past...
I train to endure much more than anyone should take...
Disguise my hurt with jokes about how words and situations
would commonly affect someone else...
Just find it much easier to shrug off my emotional baggage
by circumventing the moment myself...
I admit sometimes it's hard bearing the brunt
of circumstances you couldn't control in life...
I honestly think from like the age of like six to seventeen
I didn't have the structure or guidance to understand
what's right...
Touch and go subjects...

Elephants in the only room that you could have a seat...
And talking bout your feelings was taboo to everyone
surrounding me...
So here I am in moments playing hide and seek
with all the things I consider a trigger...
Hopefully I find my way to home base before
the problems get bigger

Settle down

Had a conversation with moms and she tried to input
wisdom on me...
Told me son...
you're getting old and and it's time to settle down...
I replied age doesn't determine time...
Hell you're sixty plus and still not married...
But nevermind...
I used to have that settle down mindset...
Just hoping I picked the right wrong person from
what was left over...
From a true believer that real love conquers all...
To unfortunately understanding misguided principles
and tainted morals...
Apparently the decree of love equals marriage was to say
the least all in my mind...
As for that happily ever after shit everyone told stories
about...
For the sake of sharing devastating details...
Let's just say they were lying...
I'm careful now in doing my own research and not just
taking word of mouth...

I've had my fair share of experiencing false representatives
at dinner tables...
So it's the YOU in the mirror that I'm more curious about...
No hiding under hats...
Standing behind walls...
Jumping in and out of character depending
on who's around to see...
But most of all for the sake of my mother's matrimonial
thoughts...
As I'm willing to give REAL LOVE a chance...
Please don't fake the role of a wife for me

Just try it

I always second guess the first thought that would
genuinely come to mind...
Convinced myself that if I shared these uncut pure emotions
you would more than likely think that I'm lying...
Past situations make it hard to believe that you are
everything that I've spoken you to be...
A queen...
Simply amazing...
The light that brightens my day...
Even ignoring the notion that you're a gift from god
made for me...
Never been loved like this before...
So maybe it's the fear that has you holding on to your
broken heart pieces as I once did...
Persuaded myself to let go of most of my heart ache and
search for the untainted piece of love that I once hid...
And wouldn't you know it...
Your hearts' ying matches absolutely flush with my hearts'
Yang...
We are the perfect balance of chemical properties mixed
to heal each other's pain...
Your smile matches the new found optimism in my once
sadden eyes...

My shoulders are no longer carrying the weight
of the world...
They are soft pillows for the moments that you just need
to cry...
You're the found belief that good things ultimately come
to those that wait...
Im reassurance to the overused used statement
"you should never lose faith"...
Together we are the divine plan of Gods' work masterfully
coming to the light...
And for once...
maybe if we stop looking for all the reasons this could
go wrong...
The chance we are willing to give it will go right

Say it ain't so

So I realized as time continues to pass...
I've made conscious efforts to treat this opportunity for love
nothing like my last...
Actually...
I may just like you way more than I should...
Normally keep these thoughts tucked deep down inside...
More so convincing myself it's for my own good...
Protecting that little piece of my heart that fights to hold
my entire world together...
Had love beat me down so many times...
I conditioned my feelings and thoughts to default
to its cool...
Yeah man whatever...
Nonchalantly going with the flow of whichever way
you think is fit...
Almost like a game of tag...
Chasing you for a touch all because I thought you said
I was it...
But oh well...
Shoulder shrugs as my pessimism reminds me it's another L
in the quest for ummm...
Maybe if I don't say the word it doesn't actually exist...

Maybe by ignoring the reality of the situation I'm afforded
more time become an optimist...
A shot in the dark of capturing what has eluded me since
I felt butterflies in my little belly...
Maybe...
Just maybe...
This time is different...
And I'm actually ready

How I grew up

I'm from the era where I legit remember when Cash Money
Records was taking over for the nine nine two thousand...
Where I seen No Limit Records consistently put out albums
every week with no problem...
Only to see them promote artist that we would never see...
Grew tired of seeing all promo of Mercedes' coming soon...
But never actually got the CD...
Introduced to that Boosie...
Felt like I was with him walking cross that dirty track...
Youngest of the camp was probably my first burnt cd...
On the first song "Shout Out"...
My thug murdered that...
At the same time of that...
I found myself playing hide n go get it with
the neighborhood girls...
Well before I had my first kiss in life...
I was ready to give up everything...
Felt like Nicole was my whole world...
Made it a point to walk up the street daily when
no one knew what it was about...
Somehow I found ways to entertain Dwayne while
she was around up until the moon came out...
I can probably say she was my first love and heartbreak

all in the same breath...

Saved my chip money to buy her Dixie cups

because I was her man...

And it wasn't a person around that could tell me

anything less...

The good ole days...

From that...

To riding three wheelers and dirt bikes up and down

the street...

Sometimes that was cool and all...

But it was mostly on the school campus where anyone

could find me...

Young earl...

Suwoo...

Manigualt...

Hot sizzle...

Just sharing a few of the names I was given...

Played from dusk til the lights cut off mid shot...

And even before seeing the basketball go in...

Not knowing if I made it or not...

You could hear me holla "game nigga"...

But this was how I grew up...

Seen my best friend sell crack and even hustle fixing

anything and everything that moved or had wheels...

Prob the smartest dummy I know from back then and

to this day still...

Growing up like this I could have easily been a product

of my habitat...

But seeing moms on drugs and even my dad the times

he was around...

Made me want something well beyond that...

Don't get me wrong though...

Im thankful for all the trials and tribulations...

And if by chance I'm ever asked...

Not without persuasion I'd truthfully admire...

Sometimes shit was bad...

But most times I've had my share of good...

But I wouldn't be the man I am today if I didn't grow up

in DA HOOD

9/4/21

Thank you for unknowingly doing the great things

you've done...

Blessings beyond measure...

Just you being you...

It's truly an honor to call you my SON...

That spelling doesn't even do justice to this feeling I get...

If I could I would spell it S U N...

A constant reminder that every day is new

and I cannot quit...

Maybe even spell it G R E A T...

To know despite whatever big moments or shortcomings...

YOURE still the greatest part of me...

J O Y...

If we are mentioning bundles when speaking of you...

Or simply KAIRO respectfully...

VICTORIOUS one...

Let your light shine through...

Purposely named for the things you're destined to do...

I finally understand the Price of GREATNESS...

It's the image of YOU

Soo…

Soo basically that last time we saw each other it was things
I wanted to say…all the thoughts in my head

I had this urge to pull you to the side and tell you
how I feel…
A warm hug…
Followed by a kiss…
Telling you I love you for real…
But was afraid of the moment…
Even more nervous of how you would take that…
Whether I was saying it for a response from you…
Or just to get it off my chest…
I wasnt exactly sure how you would react…
Make a scene out in public…
or smile while you discreetly pulled away…
From missed messages here and there…
To totally not having anything to say…
A day turn to two…
Two turn to a week…
And suddenly me spilling the beans on my feelings
doesn't seem that sweet…
But i guess the cats out the bag…
Undoubtedly I think you kinda figured so…

Im my mind it was like...

Whats the harm in sharing knowledge of something

she already know...

So there it is...

All summed up in a 200 word note...

I guess now that I've said it aloud...

I'll see how far this will go.

Can't speak

I held my breath long enough to turn purple in the face...
You have to understand exactly how long it took to do that...
Considering my dark complexion in this case...
Nevertheless I held out as long as I could...
Patiently waiting and praying you did the things
you said you would...
All the secret chats and pillow talk moments has finally
come down to this...
If by any chance the things you told me were accurate...
I can't foresee this opportunity missed...
Jokes on us though...
Although normally it would fall on me...
But the instant I saw the switch up I realized it wasn't all
it was cracked up to be...
I can...
Nope...
I will...
Nope...
Save the story telling for the weak hearted and self
proclaimed hopeless romantics...
You did...
Cool...

Just because...

Thank you...

Finally something tangible that I can understand...

Snapped out of the aww of dream chasing...

I can finally breath again

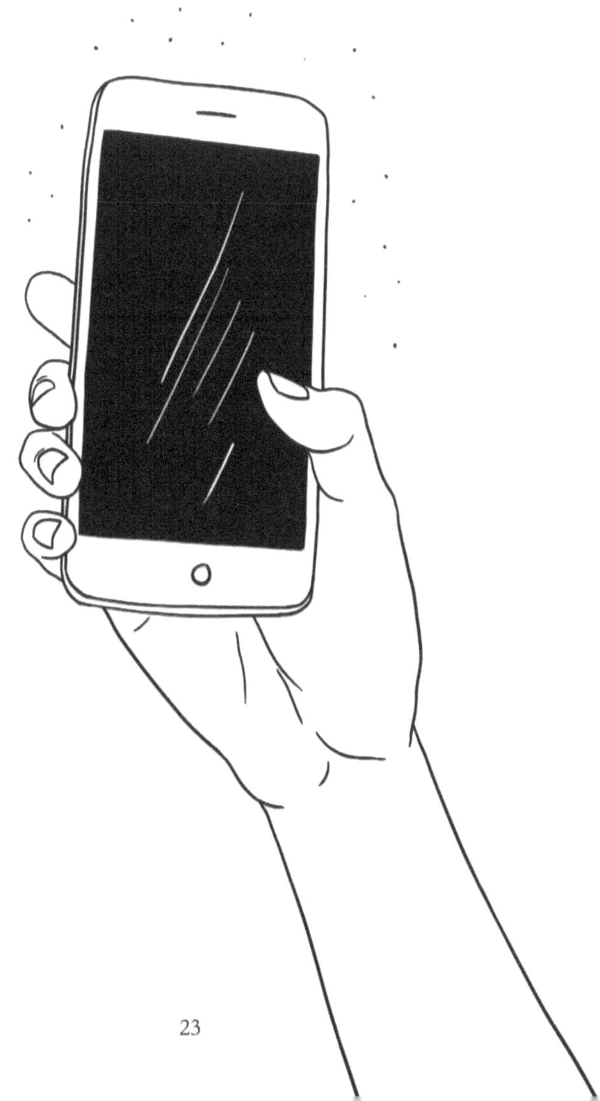

Like this

If I was the first to tell you life sucks...
Trust me it's past the point of counting and lining up
your life's ducks...
Shits as crazy as the third floor of the mental ward...
But believe me when I teeeellllllll you...
In my Kevin hart voice...
My momma said it's gonna be a bit more hard...
Jobs lost...
Bums become sponsors to those who once passed by
with their nose tilted up high...
Say man...
You have to make your sign noticeable to all the passers by...
Your small writing won't grab the attention of those
who play blind to us in need...
Ooooooohhhhhh...
I get it...
You were one of those passer bys that pretended you
could see to read...
My daughter needs uniforms for the school she's enrolled
in that I work graveyards shifts to provide...
And my promise to giving her a better life is the only reason
I'm laying my pride to the side...
I can't for the life of me bare to see her feel like I've let
her fail...

But let me guess...
You're used to kiss asses and haven't seen a moment
that you haven't prevailed...
Tisk tisk tisk...
I don't wanna be the barer of all the bad news...
But for some reason it's a small satisfaction for me that
just this one time you're not able to choose...
You have no say so if things suddenly swing your way...
And for once things in this lifetime...
It just will go LIKE THIS without you having a say

Relapse

I often jog my mental notes just to catch glimpses
of what once used to be...
End up having nightmares disguised as daydreams
replaying moments shared between you and me...
Started with smiles immediately followed by sweat oozing
from my tear ducts...
Maybe it's because I realized that in reality it's just you
and me now...
When not so many moons ago it was a legit US...
Traumatized couldn't even begin to describe the battered
state of mind I'm in...
Imagine experiencing the most excruciating pain...
Now multiply that shit times 10...
Story of my life...
And barely scratching the surface of the subject...
So to avoid the "Are you ok"..."Whats wrong" questions...
I'm forced to wear the mask of happiness while out
in public...
Joy of a clown...
Hiding the tears of a broken soul...
Now it's talks in the mirror for me...
Trying to avoid that forsaken long dark road...
Glass half full...

But that's irrelevant when the bottle's been poured over
and over again...
Being that I'm entangled in a bit of a debacle...
I'm tempted to sway to the glass half empty
as an overall win...
Find myself in constant battles each day...
Fair share of loses I've taken too...
But none pained me more than the day I realized
I had forever lost YOU

The struggle

Back when I battled depression I made it a point
to flaunt happiness out in public...
While all along hiding behind the smile of a clown secretly
shoving away my struggle...
Sure from your perspective it seemed as if things were great
in this little world of mine...
But my patience for self destruction was getting thinner
with time...
Couldn't tell you how many suicide notes I penned and
ripped up because it didn't fit the narrative of my life...
Oddly enough was tied to the idea of just hanging around
wouldn't seem right...
So in battle I went...
Carved out a few lines..
Then realized telling my story that way would
only be skin deep...
Confused how I'm widely considered the favorite...
But struggle with the same issues of the black sheep...
Thankfully I endured my parental drug addiction...
Saw dope moments die in dope moments growing up
in my house...
So it's safe to say I couldn't swallow the pill of taking
the overdose route...

But this depression still weighed heavy on my brain...
Finally came to the realization that maybe suicide
just might not be my thing...
Socially uncomfortable as I feel the smell of life's defeat
is escaping my pores...
But I'll let you in on a small secret of mine...
If ever y'all didn't see or hear from me?...
Im with God dealing with this monster behind closed doors

Depression is an ugly monster that needs not shoed away...
there's always someone willing to help and one call away.

Im not a poet…

Before I go any further I just wanna say I'm not a poet
I just needed an outlet for my thoughts as we all do
Just figured it was therapeutic to write but sometimes
it clearly evolves you
Before you go to thinking it
Let me be clear I'm not a poet
I'm just slightly metaphoric with the phrases and witty
with my penmanship
Now Clearly you can see I'm definitely not a poet
I don't go to deep with writing
But barely scratch the surface of my artistic creativity
A few lines that rhyme when writing here and there
Most of the times its complaints we can all relate to
and about how life is just so unfair
Nothing poetic about that
Right?
Especially when I find myself explaining love and passion
when I'm emotionally unavailable to whomever I cross paths
And here you are saying I'm something like a poet

while I'm everything opposite of that
I would like to be considered as a person with the secret
obsession of writing my inner most thoughts that I'm to
uncomfortable to verbalize but willing to share in ink
Hmmm maybe that does make me almost poetic
when you really sit back and think
I guess I am a poet

Child Support

Let me in Jody

She told me she hate me in her best Evette vocals...
So I smiled because I knew exactly what came next...
But to my surprise it was a genuine hate for my actions...
So upon refusal of me taking her down...
I smirked and said bet...

Keys off the dresser...
Metaphoric Black & Mild on the tip of my lips...
Decided I'll spend my day bending corners since my baby
momma decided to trip...
I'm just a baby boy...

But no scene plays out like the others...
I figured it was her in her feelings for a second...
Then somehow she decided to take it a little further...
Now Im in court playing baby daddy...
All because she wanted me to stop playing baby daddy...

And be there morning noon and night...
Can't say I blame her for feeling this way...
But figured she would let a nigga have time
to get himself right...

Nine months came faster than either one of us expected...
And now all the ups and downs we've encountered
got you feeling like you regret it...
In my ear talking bout I would have done such and such
if I would have seen this coming...

Had to bite my tongue to not call you everything under
the sun but a woman...
Almost stepped outta character and showed you just
how a NIGGA could be...
But I'm empathetic and understanding to most but only
to a certain degree...

No problem though...
We've been back and forth...
And it's been going on for some months...
So regardless of how much you feel you hate my guts...

I know it's only because I haven't given in to what
you want...

Writing it in...

I used to pen notes to myself trying to make sense of where
I'm at in life...
Found myself ripping those up because seeing it on paper
just didn't seem right...
Telling myself every decision made was geared towards
the greater good...
But standing in the mist of everything I would change
some things if I could...
First change would be disregarding the silly notion
of looking back...
I can definitely do without the constant reminders of where
I went left trying to do everything right...
Maybe I could replace that Hennessy with water from that
shhh don't mention it night...
Yeah...definitely a stroll down a dark alley that I would
like to forget...
And by no means was it the worst...
I'm just shamed to admit I enjoyed it...
Can't clean the tainted memories of my not so long
ago past...
So I guess a purpose of writing this was to see it and
make it my last...
Fake forgiveness as I read through the bold letters printed

for everyone to see...

Force fed the reality of everything I've grown to be...

Just tearing up the papers don't mean those sentences are
suddenly run ons or fragments of the truth...

Maybe if you find those slightly tarnished crumbled pieces
of paper it'll show the fragmented sentences are just pieces
of you

I'm that

Not to toot my own horn...
But beep beep...
I'm something like that shit you talk about late at night
with your friends...
I'm most definitely part of the drunk conversation before
the night ends...
I may not be HIM...
But a dream deferred...
Nothing like the things you've seen before...
But close to everything you've previously heard...
That excitement after midnight...
But embarrassed to admit before noon...
I'm that wink in the mirror when you know you're linking
up soon...
A breath of fresh air out here in these Covid streets...
That feeling after you've experienced court side seats...
Can't tell me nothing...
The thought of feeling you've finally made it...
But play with me wrong...

I'm that long awaited taken spot that's suddenly vacant...

That wish you made that never came true...

That on the way text that never came through...

I'm your thoughts when you find yourself overthinking...

But could be that 3rd cup of liquor before you realized

you were over drinking...

More than a moment...

I could be a lifetime of happiness or grief...

Depends on how you handle me...

I'm either your headache or peace...

I'm all your efforts wrapped in one.

A friend in ME

Once had this crazy experience with someone I would now call the worlds greatest friend...but don't get it twisted by far...was definitely the furthest title from my mind when we met way back when...I mean I was hesitant...yet curious to approach because of the facial expressions when looking towards me...hell before my initial approach I detoured to another mirror to get a glance for a visual of exactly what this person would see...breath checked then washed my hands and proceeded all while nervous to my core...prep talked "it's now or never man...if you're really gonna do this...what the hell are you waiting for?"...so I gassed myself up and put on the biggest smile...don't get me wrong...yeah I've met a ton of people before...but not someone this interesting in quite a while...a touch of shyness mixed with confidence in the person that they are meant to be...classified smart because they only showed to whose looking what was meant to individually see...and as the conversation initiated I sensed his dopeness and easily spotted his wit...I'm quite certain before initial contact...neither of us imagined the results we would get...so much in common...as we chatted things became more clear to the naked eye...a long blink as I thought to myself this is one heck of a guy...as we went to depart we both gave a head nod in agreement laughing at the crazy things we do and see... and at an instant...the title transitioned from just the stranger in the mirror...to the GREATEST friend in ME

A 👑 🏉

I can remember you always being the buzz of the ball...

Whether it was a turn up at a party...

Or just a family event in the yard...

You were the vital part of it all...

You possessed the energy that was contagious

to say the lease...

Not lacking in any category...

You were a beauty and a beast...

Confident enough to show out...

But humble enough to make everyone else comfortable

in your space...

Understanding and supportive of your friends no matter

of the case...

Always looked out for your circle...

Loving and caring for those close to you...

A ride or die friend when needed...

Such a queen B thing to do...

Despite all the happy moments with you...

I can't lie but this one stings...

I have to accept God had other plans for you...

So he saw fit it was time to get your wings...

Long live Queen B

Love where art thou...

I always wondered what happened to the spare pieces
of my heart once it was broken...
See I've been in and out of some great,
some not so great relationships...
But the ultimate demise of things came down to the lines
of communication not being completely open...
One person said they loved me...
And like so many I fell in suite...
Besides...
It's common to respond to the simple notion of I love you
with a smile and I love you too...
Meant in the moment or not...
The words escaped the depth of my mouth...
Truth of the matter is I think in comparison to you...
I forgot what love was about...
I legit feel like my heart shattered and the things
that made up real love for me shattered as well...
Friendship in one piece...trust in another...
and loyalty went to hell...
Now I'm the gate keeper of that...
Loyal to my own needs and happiness from that point
in my life...
Even when I thought I was happy...

I messed things up trying to make sure it was right...

The irony of that...

Invisible hoops...

Questionable situations...

All to prove to myself this is finally it...

And any moment of uncertainty I'll challenge myself

to quit...

Find fault in my future because I'm not quite over my past...

Secretly hoping the Bible verse comes to light where my first

is my last...

Tattooed over my heart...

In the most literal sense possible...

Maybe it's right...

Maybe it's wrong...

But at the rate I'm going...

For anything to develop I gotta know

Runaway thougths

If I let my imagination get away from me I know
I'll be chasing you forever...
So I planned to drop this anchor right here since
I don't foresee any moment being better...

At first glance I seen us running away hand in hand...
Visions of you at your happiest and me being your
ideal man...
Blinked twice just to assure myself that this was a mirage
of everything that wouldn't be...

The obscured mirror imagery made it seemed like you
were actually chasing me...
Even in my wildest dreams that scene isn't even worth
the thought...

To fathom such an improbable connection would mean
somewhere along the line I softened your heart...
Urkel to your Laura Winslow...
Flowers...
Candy...

Dismay romantic gestures...
And still feel like I'm wearing you down baby...
But as the darkness off truth over shadows my visions...

I feel it's best I get a handle of these runaway thoughts
I've been having lately

Recycled Love

In remembrance of your past you find yourself looking
for the next victim...
Oops I mean person to light your candle...
And wide eyes shut his puppy love is evidently
more than you can handle...

But you continue to just go with the flow...
Refuse to acknowledge this as just a rebound lust...
You're here to see this thing out for as far as it can go...
Holding his hand while imagining what was once before...
His consistency through his actions has you wondering
should you be doing more...

Bartering with material things because his physical
isn't up to par with your visual needs...
Masking your disgust of how you're being loved by him
for your emotional greed...
All he wants is everything you have...

I mean flaws and red flags popping up in every
random moment...
Yet you're just out here recycling the love for your ex
with anyone who's willing to condone it

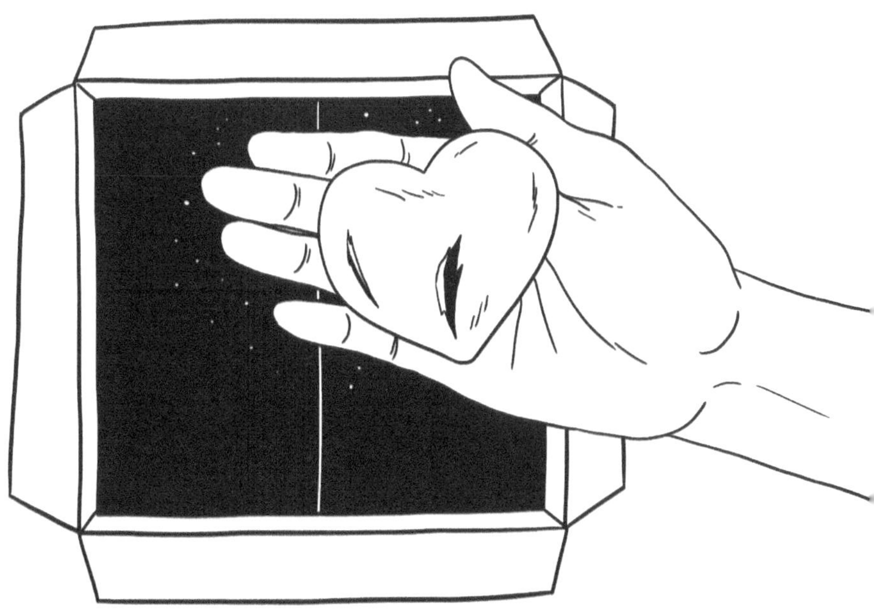

Wrong person

For quite some time now I've been having this settle down
feeling overwhelming my conscious...
With faith in what's for me is for me quote...
I'm hoping I don't accidentally pursue the wrong person
for the right responses...

Tried pleading with myself and telling my heart
to be patient...
I want that SEE YOURSELF IN THE MIRROR LOVE
out in the public...
So it's no masks and all naked truth is what I'm facing...

After seasons of drought hoping this love flower
would bud...
I soon came to the realization you can't pray for rain
and be disgusted by the mud...

Battles

I couldn't find the words so I started with building blocks...
Laid a solid foundation then it was piece by piece...
All the way to the rooftop...
See how tall I am now...
Hopefully this jenga puzzle won't fall before I grab
your attention...
It seems like my heart skips a beat every time your name
is mentioned...
The tune of butterflies by micheal jackson dancing
through my mind...
Crazy how you spend your whole life looking for love...
Yet when love is banging at your door you suddenly
don't have the time...
Shut in...
Wall up...
Omarion icebox song playing on repeat...
All while I'm screaming to the top of my lungs...
I'm literally your number fan please please pick me...
Ignored and overlooked...
I guess you really don't know love at first glance...
So I stood up and raised my hand hoping this time
hoping that you would give this love thing a chance...

It's you

Everything in a moments glance...

Deep breathes and nervous shakes upon the sight of you...

This that shit that makes you think life could end

and you will be fulfilled...

I mean it's not moments ever fathomed that compares...

Couldn't for the life of you see myself anywhere on gods

green earth besides here...

Yeah...completed the circle of life all in like 2 mins

of circling my thoughts...

You're the exact embodiment of what we call gods

best work of art...

More poise then Mona Lisa...

And the 16th chapel couldn't even compare...

If we are being sincere about things...

You're definitely that chill people get when stepping into

the night air...

The overwhelming feeling when things seem just so right...

That fraction of time between dusk and dawn when we see

the transition from day to night...

Special or gifted...

Whatever suits you best...

You're that marathon love

Forever got my heart racing trying to be my best...

And me...

Yeah little me...

I'm just happy to be on the receiving end...

Hell I feel like sometimes I'm that message that you refuse

to send...

Not worthy of time or effort...

Yet a conscious thought in your world...

What's this

I think somewhere along the line of us doing this love thing
you ignored the together part...
I at times feel like you say the words but only give me
a piece of your heart...
It's easy to do the things convenient or when it costs little
to none of your time...
All along I'm bending over backwards and making time stop
to show you how much I'm seriously trying...
Realize instead of being like bae I got you and actually
having me instead you non threaten to break up right...
How could you love someone as much as you say you do
and not even put up a fight...
Just answering the phone alone proves nothing...
Hell even staying on through the loud talks and
disagreements aren't even something to brag about...
Actions behind those words means so much more than
just talking it out...
This isn't the first time we have been far apart
from seeing eye to eye...
But the change in this time from last time before I let my
emotions get the best of me I'm ok with just saying bye...
I won't beg you for anything...
As you would say you're not asking me to...
And I should never have too...

So simply put...

The things I need to grow together I'll just politely ask you...

And asking more than twice seems to close to a beg...

You want a ring...

I want a wife...

Make it make sense in your head

Tired

Facts are facts...

Let's call them like we see it...

In this age of America when it comes to being

actually black...

Everyone would rather not be it...

Grant it we find humor in things just to get us by...

Being black is dangerous and lit all at the same time...

Probably the whitest of lies...

I'd prefer not to be hunted...

Gunned down like and animal in the street...

And even if I manage to hold on for dear life...

I'm made out to everything under the sun except for

whom I'm meant to be...

A father...

A brother...

A son...

Not even depicted as a normal human being...

Characterized as a monster and not the victim that

everyone is clearly seeing...

Kneeled on and not for...

I guess my life really doesn't matter...

But the fact that I'm suddenly a monster after you've

blatantly attacked me...

That shit only makes it sadder...

Suddenly my past regardless of the situation makes me

out to be the scum of the earth...

Correct me if I'm wrong...

But in the Bible doesn't it say "he who's without sin cast

the stone first"?...

Not arguing that I'm perfect...

Hell not even saying I'm better than some...

But how many times does every black person in this world

have to fall victim to a white man protected by privilege

while carrying a loaded gun?

I wanted so bad to be what you felt you wanted in your life...

But no matter the one man show I give you...

I just can't seem to get right...

You say jump and I ask how high...

Apparently I'm just not quite high enough...

But I will do for now...

Especially with the status of the world right now...

Things are kinda tough...

Heartbreak

I was wondering how come this thing I harbor for you
is impossible to see...
Like no matter the effort I put forth...
Here stands an invisible me...
Looked pass...
Ran over...
Sometimes just a stand in for the attention you need...
All along fooling myself with the hope you'll finally get it...
While my heart constantly bleeds...
They say fools fall in love...
And I told myself I wouldn't be him anymore...
Yet I opened Pandora's box willingly...
All while knowing what was in stored...
Heartbreak...
Agony...
Days alone...
And nights with not a moment of rest...
Only comfort I find in the pain is knowing
that I gave it my best...
They say go big or don't go...
The quote is something along those lines...
While doing my best to just cope...
Told myself every wound eventually heals in time

Making it through the rain ensures a moment of sun

Kickboxing

Find myself taking chances in this thing called life...

Funny I'm suddenly kickboxing...

Definitely not used to being combative with my thoughts...

But mentally in a fight or flight situation it's no point

to the dodge the aggressive nature of my heart...

Got me tugging on strings...

Found myself tryna plead before things came to blows...

Besides...

It's only the first round and from the right hook...

Upper cut...

Round house combination...

I'm in wondering should I restrain from telling her

the obvious things she already knows...

Suppress the moment...

Opposed to the fact of thinking small and staying inside

the box...

I feel all the pressure as the last seconds

of the round winds down...

And all I can hear is the moving hands on the clock...

Figured it was no contest as the battle seemed

to already been won...

Strangely an unusual quarrel right before the final bell

has rung...

Nothing violent because it's just not how things should go...
However I was asked to step out of the ring and watch
my opponent spar alone from the front row...

LETTING YOUR GUARD DOWN IS HARD...

Lost

Couldn't focus on the path straight to destiny...

Figured it was something I was missing...

Only to find out it was just the fact that I had lost me...

Somewhere in between the start of it all ...

And this point I'm paused at...

So now I'm diggin through the rubbish trying to find that...

Day one was simple...

One step forward followed by the next...

But it was the complications of day two that I was pushed

to be my best...

And not just the best of me...

But the best of them all...

And with odds like that stacked against any man...

He's destined to fall...

So down goes Frazier...

And back up on day six thousand five hundred seventy...

Curtains open and wallah...

It's the new and improved version of me...

Two point something...

Then it's off to the next phase of this life long hike...

Ahead it's high mountains and low valleys...

With not a resting point in sight...

Blew pass the moments you're supposed to stop

and take it all in...

So now I find myself back tracking to catch it all..

Over and over again...

Impeding the progress of what life has to offer...

Coincidentally in one of those moments

I was looking back...

I subsequently lost HER...

But as they say...

The show must go on...

And onward I went...

So far from the peak of it all and already contemplating

the descent

It's an uphill battle...keep going!!

Ying Yang

I remember I had a strange addiction for self inflicted pain... what's even more odd is that somehow heartbreak would turn on a light switch in my brain...the more I endure... the better I get...was like that fight or flight feeling exposed through my wrist...penmanship on a hunnit with every thought of suffering through tragedy...as I hold back tears... strangely I'm somewhat happy that you're actually mad with me...finally a push to dig deeper and share what's within... so immediately after the disastrous encounter I'm forced to begin...for starters...I'm sorry...at least that's how I feel while transitioning through these thoughts...not so much for the interaction...but for what I know are the desires of my heart...I'm a what people would call "can't get right"... no matter how much effort I show...I manage to somehow lose at life...lose at love...and eventually I'm lost completely... but even with all the Ls I'm willing to take...I won't let this loser feeling defeat me...through the pain I'm adapting to be great...through the hopeless moments I'm gravitating more towards faith...and in the darkness I'm finding ways to make my own silver lining...while everyone else sees the most inopportune moment...my eyes can only see this as perfect timing...this is balance outweighed in the universe that said this thing shouldn't be...this is the ying to the yang...this is that YOU TO ME

I'm scared

I'm scared
And this is by far one of the hardest things to admit...
All my life I was told men don't cry or show emotion...
And as a man it's the hardest thing for me to get...
I've cried in dark rooms for moments I know I could
never get back...
I've even went out on the limb and shared my feelings...
Then wondered did I really NEED to do that...
But I'm definitely scared...
And this isn't just an ordinary fear of mine...
It's that daunting haunting feeling that I can't seem
to get out of my mind...
You ever been bullied by time?
Always seeming like you have to much on your hand
but never quite enough?...
Crazy how we have all the time in the world until things
in life start to get tough...

This what I want

I don't like asking so I mention things in hopes you grasp
the concept...
It's like I throw out detailed and specific clues so you don't
accidentally go left...
And even if missed the first time around I do my best
to sneak it in back...
Pssssst...I hope you're listening because this is yet
another attempt to help you get things on track...
I'm very aware that even I if wanted you to it's no way
you could read minds...
So I'll just keep hope alive that your vision gets better
with time...
I can admit I'm a bit difficult...
You can blame my let downs in the life that i live...
But on the opposite end of that...
I promise I won't ask you for anything that I'm not willing
to give...
Please save those in the moment vibes because it sounds
good at the time...
Trust I'm rarely ever excited about it knowing it's just
another "I GOT YOU BAE" line...
Or that "ANYTHING FOR YOU BOO"...
Especially when I know it's just words...

I need you to have that same energy showing me...
To go along with those phrases I've heard...
They say ACTIONS speak volumes...
Meaning words are just the start of the tasks...
Summarizing that IF YOU really got me like that...
Then I shouldn't have NOT ONE reason to ask

Tried

So I tried to be the best of me for a change...

And figured when it all fails it's my head to blame...

My heart is usually conflicted and I'm almost always
ignoring the signs...

Guess I got to carried away with the thought of me and you
becoming an WE and US in my mind...

Regardless of the fact I shared my wants and desires
at the beginning of day one...

Assumed you would be down for it all due to the fact
you embraced it and when faced you didn't run...

Surely you backed off for a second...

But it didn't halt your return...

And silly me oh silly me...

I was patiently waiting for you to be the one...

Didn't think past the moment because I believe in dancing
in the spotlight...

Figured so many times I had been wrong...

And even with the hiccups this moment seemed to be
just right...

Blame my want to find HER...

Or my want to get past losing what I thought was
my future...

Either route you decide to take...

I assumed this version of the story would ultimately
suit you...
It's your choice in the matter...
You can pick the road frequently taken...
Or the one that's less traveled...
I'll wait patiently for your arrival since I've noticed
you gassing up...
And if by chance you detour or pit stop en route...
I'll just add this potential joy ride to another victim
to my dumb luck

It's time

If you don't get it now...just know that's it's not too late

to start...

Hopefully the words that you hear or read from this point

forward changes your mental and touches your heart...

We as a people are under attack from what was created

by those that was less human than god intended...

It's still unjust rules and biased behavior regardless

of the root of the problem being quote unquote amended...

Never have we once been treated the same as our less

melanin counterparts...

But always expected to turn the other cheek instead of

advocating for more of our deserved rights when things

fall apart...

Guilty by the pigmentation of our skin...

As if we had a choice in the color wheel...

I tell you this...

As an American...

I mean an anglo Saxon must be nice to be able to come

and go as you feel...

No reason to look over your shoulder or wonder if you

will be stopped just because your shade is shaded...

Sometimes makes me question if you believe your black

is as beautiful as the words when stated...

America...

Land of the privileged...

Home of the colonizers who believe WE are a threat

to their power structure...

So it's their vision to divide and destroy by any means

when they find a reason to touch us...

Sure all lives matter...

But that's spoken on a much broader scale...

It never seizes to amaze me that those posts aren't made

and words aren't uttered until it's videos of black people

protesting this living hell...

It's not a FUCKING conundrum...

SIMPLY DO WHAT THE FUCK IS RIGHT...

I guess it's not a running joke anymore when we talk about

"ALL MY LIFE I HAD TO FIGHT"...

Bullshit if I ever seen it...

A venomous hate from a tormented past...

I know George Floyd wasn't the first...

But with everything our ancestors ancestors fought for...

WE CAN COME TOGETHER

AND MAKE IT THE LAST

No bars

No mentions for what once was...

I start thinking bout the right now...

Seen visions of the future and gave you advice every time

you asked how...

Would think I'm poetic justice on principle of the things

we normally go through...

It's crazy when you think about the fact that someone

is actually attempting to get to know you...

See this is what we fear...

The unexpected and unknown of possibilities...

But what if we disregard the what if's and just lived

in the moment...

Find yourself being like I would but...

Yea we get it...

Your mental just wont condone it...

Think to much...

On some captain America shit...

Can't save the man in the mirror...

But consciously chasing the ghosts of the past...

I'm sure if I believed all cliches...

Yea he's who's wins right now would somehow finish last...

False hope...

Learned that you get second chances...

But opportunities are legit once in a lifetime...
And if by chance I don't seize the moment I wouldn't be
in my right mind...
Don't knock twice...
Hell if you pass the second time I'm grabbing an elbow...
Prob the wildest dumb shit I've heard is when you know
you know...
But all guessing aside...
Moving according to your spiritual vibrations...
I'm that aforementioned second chance but rare third
opportunity because of my patience we won't mention...
Decide what makes more sense for the things you see putting
that smile on your face...
And while you're smiling and thinking about it...
Laugh and lie and say in this moment even if it was
for a split second you didn't see my face

No settling

My competitive nature wouldn't allow me to settle...

So in search for you I fought the complacent feeling

to strive and do better...

Match made in my mental because when I followed my heart

things became more complicated and less simple...

From contradictory emotions that once led me

to an empty bed...

I learned to recognize the bull and swerve through

those circumstantial feelings instead...

Now here I am...

Pivotal moment of me stepping into my guiding light...

Refuse to believe the cliche love is blind...

When i know in actuality it aids in sight...

Highlighted flaws we learn to accept...

Filled gaps we may sometimes miss...

We were trained to like people because of something...

But grow to love them regardless...

And this is my testimony to what I've worked to become...

Diligently crafting my heart for her as she is the only one...

Detailed in every facet so when presented things

are just outside of perfection...

Flares

I can't even front like the possibility never crossed
my thoughts...
Just told myself it was time to uncage my mending heart...
Feelings on my sleeve and expressed purposely...
Disregard to the common result of that always hurting me...
But with love being a gamble...
That makes life a casino...
And with free space and time...
I unscrambled the puzzle pieces and it turned to be
I in gee ohh/go mode...(slow down)
(But) Forward progress with the actions set in motion...
Precise with my words that illustrates my devotion...
See this is definitely me...
No representative or representation of something I'm not...
From my gut feelings to my deepest thoughts I'm here
giving you all that I got...
Mistake perhaps...
Or purposely being real...
No blindfolded intentions...
This is how finally being seen feels...
Attentive and affectionate...
Considerate to show I care...
(Funny how I)Found myself tryna light the candle...
Just to see it's only a flare

Scratch paper

Scratch paper for these random thoughts
plaguing my stability
Can't understand with all that's been shown
you're somehow still not feeling me
Subconsciously battling that leave you behind notion
reoccurring on my mental
But over the course of life I've grown to learn walking away
just isn't that simple
You're hit with the what ifs
Why didn't I
Or I should have tried harder
All followed by the negativity of you feeling like why bother
Energy should be reciprocated
And when it's not it dies
Looking for the rhythmic pattern in this case
What happened to that vibe
Was so in tune once before
As if the world was finally playing the soundtrack to our life
Then randomly a skipped beat and nothing's going right
I'm up
You're down
You're right
I'm left

What was once a solo act turned duet
Suddenly became all about yourself
In and out of the spotlight with you
Crazy how quickly in no time things can change
Reminded myself this is only scratch paper to weather
the storms in my brain

Pump your brakes

I guess it's me being more so myself...
Glances in the rear view mirror for whatever seems
to be left...
Old traditions passed over for these new age games...
How is it possible me giving you attention somehow turns
into me being lame...
Do my best to be nothing like others as I'm quick
to proclaim...
But despite your assumption of attachment or me moving
to fast...
I'm driving with precaution all in the right lane...
But it's brake lights you're wanting...
So with the emergency flashers,
I slam them and catch the shoulder...
Sorry but I was enjoying the views at 45...
Usually what happens when you get a bit older...
No time for fast pace living...
Purposely avoid the left lane...
Guess in hindsight while driving...
I expected the exit after the light had changed...
Excuse myself for wanting to be sure I was following
the GPS...
Vowed no left turns or left lanes,
was finally just tryna do the right thing at best

I waited...

Laughed because I thought it was all just some
sick bad joke...
But to my surprise it was the final thread pulled
from my last little bit of hope...
Patience she said...
So I waited...
Time went by that produced thoughts that because
of my position I was forbidden to share...
And despite the situation I felt like this punishment
was not only stupid but most definitely unfair...
But still...I waited
Reminded her I asked to be told her thoughts and concerns
about it all on day one...
Rather accept it all in the beginning because I know seeing
the love of your life walk away is the least bit of fun...
And yet...I waited
Treated her like she was still the most important person
in my life...
I figured it would be foolish to treat her any different
and somehow mess up twice...
Tick tick...I am waiting
Hours passed that turned to days,
those days ended just shy of a month

Finally a text response,
admitting the waiting game was only a front...
It's here...
Knew the instance things happened you undoubtedly
wanted out...
But played the let me think about it to see exactly
how things would eventually come about...
Showed you it was a foolish mistake that in a millions years
I wouldn't even think about doing again...
And yet you still decided to walk away like this
is some unforgivable sin...
Not perfect as nothing in life is or ever will be...
While I can't change the past, but only make better
of the person you will see...
And it's decision time...no more waiting
Prayed for this to work and vowed to do whatever
to help you feel secure and believe...
Yet my pleas of, I LOVE YOU...I WANT THIS
FOREVER...had no barring of you still deciding to leave...
She said wait...
She left...

Patience is definitely a virtue,
but sometimes being patient for the wrong thing
or person would eventually hurt you...
LIFE

Came Up Short

So many efforts to be everything I thought you wanted... somehow I still fell short...being just another stupid man and unfortunately for me letting my head confuse the feelings of my heart...I definitely should have known better from the very first time we met...on sight the connection was stupid crazy...I mean as crazy as crazy can get...from that meeting not a day passed without waking up to the sunrise on your beautiful face...even when it was dark and cloudy outside I still seen that precious glow from your amazing grace...and it's not a second I would return of what we shared...but foolish me oh so so foolish of me...I didn't treat your once broken heart fair...gave attention to things that couldn't hold a match to your light...and because I was dumb and dumber...now I'm in a fight for my life...wanting what I lost with no cause but my own selfish actions...and I'm quick to raise my hand and take blame for everything that has happened...bent down on my knees pleading for you to give this another go...hoping that my character you grew to love ultimately phased out the things you've come to know...no doubt I would be ignorant to expect you to suddenly be blind to it...but hoping you see past me being what you told me upfront was a huge fear... it's no words in the dictionary thats more than my actions of showing you I'm here...I'm upset at myself to say the lease because I know with you it's where I'm destined to be...I can adamantly and honestly admit since May 7 I've strived to be the best version of me...and yet I still found ways to not be so adequate...but as I plea my case for your heart...Ive dropped everything in the background to present to you the best version of me anyone can get.

Love has shown me hurt...
love has shown me abandonment...
but most of all...
love has shown me someone that's heaven sent.

Even in Disneyland I couldn't imagine
a future without you.

Black History Forever

I read the sign...it clearly said additional parking behind the building...but for some reason I wanted to be seen and park in the front like everyone else...for so many years I've been told to park in the back...sit in the back...go to the back...and quite frankly I'm tired of being the last person seen or heard... because I'm forever in the back...when ever did the plants in back get any sunshine?...think about it...or even the clothes in the back of the closet make it to the public's eye?...for once I wanna be seen...heard...you know like the people in the front...I guess timing is everything...and being on time means you get to be in the front...you get to choose...hell sometimes you're even chosen...and I know all the first will be last and last will be first talk...but got damn...how long do I have to wait...my grandest of elders did enough back seat riding for all of us...so I declare this the year of the coupe...ain't no back seat...he'll I won't even accept being a passenger this month... especially if it's some driving me Daisy shit happening... and pardon my cursing...not my typical genre of language... guess it's the NIGGA in the back coming to the front not knowing how to act because I'm very seldom heard...no more quiet whispers about what I would do if I was in the front...or how I would handle things when I legit have people behind me...this is my moment...I am that dream the king had...that seed that was planted in the concrete that wasn't expected to grow...I don't even think my ancestors fathomed the thought of this...no closed fist in representation of what my people stand for or believe in...I'm the face of it all...I am the perseverance through the storm...the sunlight that shines after those darkest nights...deeply rooted in my culture and emancipation of what once bonded us...I am not history...in fact I am the present and continuously making moments...I am ME...I am YOU...I am what makes this month GREAT.

Mental jog

Had these dope thoughts circling my cerebellum so of course I wanted to share...or maybe I'm just speaking nominally as the ambiance of fresh weed smoke possessed the calming in the air...beanie seigel shit...yeah I'm high off life...wondering if this integrated procession could mean ultimately we would all win...while some agree with protesting bans...We should find refuge in seeking savior of man to repent for all our sins...a movement of this nature is by far the greatest foray against the devil...just thinking with all things considered it's really us against him when the dust settles...prepared for war once we can on cue regurgitate passages as if it was an acting script... with each battle encountered you have verses from annals of the holy wreath...no casualties...because Calvary...it's in the book of Luke if you wanna know...With a moment like this... faith is proven fact that nothing's imperceptible.

Valentines Day

I love love but refuse to let myself fall vulnerable to yet another situationship...so pardon my middle finger to the thought of letting those forbidden words cross the seal of my forsaken lips...so yeah...I'm not out here vying for attention...or pleading my case for some semi thoughtful... unemotional...generic words on piece of card stock...like on the cool it's no way I'm believing that those same 27 words mass produced makes each person that receive them and I quote "heart stop"...and y'all out here gassing people up when in reality it's not the thought that counts but the choice of dinner reservations and finally receiving that gift that didn't quite make the Christmas list...but lucky for you this man made holiday allows the cheaters...slackers...and half effort makers a whole day to act like your thoughts aren't being so remiss...but don't let me deter your heart though...wouldn't want your moment of bliss spoiled...or blatantly interrupt that need for passion...and when it blossoms from lustful thoughts to actually love...I'm melted by moments when the magic shit happens...so applaud the pure hearts who stand for and behind the things that they say...but cheers to all you suckers who fell for the fiasco of Valentine's Day

"Ain't no CUPID bih"

How you see me

Working on a public image...

just tryna be what the people have come to expect...

unknowingly growing as the common villain...

so chasing visions of my nightmares...

Seems that's all I have left...

done wrong so many times...

doing right is blasphemy and a curse...

but when you find yourself overly neglected...

you tend to forget your actual worth...

trading time for material praises...

affection for random words...

faith tested situationships...

far less than what anyone deserves...

and while you're thinking hero...

couldn't save the mirror image even if I tried...

influenced by my budding potential...

Dr. Jekyll potion keep at bay Mr. Hyde...

but in the moments of feeling gifted...

reminded of responsibilities attached to the GREATS...

Clark Kent or Bruce Wayne...

not by choice...

but by FATE

Remind me

Sometimes we lose track of the goal set in place
when we first met...
Remind me of the reasons not asking for your number
would be my biggest regret...
Keep me honest and loyal to the things I promised
on those late night calls...
Remind me of the reasons for you I'm ready to risk it all...
Hold me to the notion of marriage until death do us part...
Remind me to never let my mind play tricks on my heart...
Hug me in moments you feel I'm in need of affection...
Remind me with your touch how deep is our connection...
Talk me up in moments you see I'm feeling down...
Remind me of all the reason I keep you around...
Frequently and randomly do all the things you see above...
And I promise I won't need a reminder of why I fell in love

Not another Love Poem

I didn't wanna just write some mushy words
that cross my mind when I think about you...
But I do want to share my feelings about us
that I hold very true...
I want you as a lover...
But more so as a friend...
I want that infinity bond with you...
One that will never end...
Love stories like ours aren't built to last long...
So it's my hope that we prove all the naysayers wrong...
1st official Valentine together...
Hopefully followed by a million more...
So I give my time...
My heart...
And every ounce of love you can handle...
To you and only you Mi Amor

Happy Love Day

Make it Last

Enamored with the chase of dissolving all the what ifs
that comes with the possibility of us...
Praying that it's not quicksand disguised as something solid
as we are trying to build on love and trust...
Hate to make the same mistake the first time around...
Falling in love solo yet again...
Especially when I vowed to hold onto this little piece
of heart I have left for emergency use only when I know
she has fully let me in...
So tired of arguing with myself about myself trying to see it
from someone else's perspective...
Fancy thoughts of being IT...
Expensive hopes of sharing life...
Followed by empty bottles of pain easers...
Chastising myself with why I can't get it right?...
Indecent proposals text messages that you wish
you never received...
And I wish I never sent...
All to be followed up with a
"this my last message for real" text...
Asking "if you really loved me?"...
Then doubling back confessing my undying love
once again...

Finally realizing my toxic trait is being an on again off again hopeless romantic...

Out here loving love at its highest peak...

Then somehow look around and suddenly panic...

Am I not enough?...

Am I doing too little for you...

Or unintentionally am I doing too much?...

With optimism for a real future...

Cautiously disregarding my past...

All things summed up to one question...

Can we make this LOVE last?

Growing up in small town Bayou Goula, LA, Deshaun Price found an outlet at an early age with writing. What started as raps with friends over random instrumentals, turned into heartfelt poetry minus the beats. Inspired by music at times, as a hopeless romantic he writes about love found, as well as love lost and moments in between. Due to the unwillingness to verbally share his feelings, this is a collection of notes he penned in the wake of all those life events.